SQUELCH PROCEDURES

MLA CHERNOFF

GORDON HILL
PRESS

Edited by Shane Neilson
Cover image by MLA Chernoff
Cover and book design by Jeremy Luke Hill
Proofreading by Carol Dilworth
Set in Superclarendon
Printed on Mohawk Via Felt
Printed and bound by Arkay Design & Print

LIBRARY AND ARCHIVES CANADA CATALOGUING IN PUBLICATION

Title: (Squelch procedures) / (MLA Chernoff).
Names: Chernoff, MLA, 1991- author.
Description: Poems.
Identifiers: Canadiana (print) 2021021645X | Canadiana (ebook) 20210216522 |
    ISBN 9781774220320 (softcover) | ISBN 9781774220337 (PDF) |
    ISBN 9781774220344 (HTML)
Classification: LCC PS8605.H4635 S68 2021 | DDC C811/.6—dc23

ONTARIO ARTS COUNCIL
CONSEIL DES ARTS DE L'ONTARIO
an Ontario government agency
un organisme du gouvernement de l'Ontario

Gordon Hill Press gratefully acknowledges the support of the Ontario Arts Council.

Gordon Hill Press respectfully acknowledges the ancestral homelands of the Attawandaron, Anishinaabe, Haudenosaunee, and Métis Peoples, and recognizes that we are situated on Treaty 3 territory, the traditional territory of Mississaugas of the Credit First Nation.

Gordon Hill Press also recognizes and supports the diverse persons who make up its community, regardless of race, age, culture, ability, ethnicity, nationality, gender identity and expression, sexual orientation, marital status, religious affiliation, and socioeconomic status.

Gordon Hill Press
130 Dublin Street North
Guelph, Ontario, Canada
N1H 4N4
www.gordonhillpress.com

I am tired of the diarrhea rhetoric, OK! you cast it off and it lands again as demagogy in embroidered shirts. No one wants my memorial pain, OK! Caught between two enemas and a friend, the library where all the zombies I had unearthed had given way but other perverts of delirium still emerge. When I think of memory, OK! I break its head.
—
Erín Moure, *Kapusta*

The monument's action is not memory but fabulation. We write not with childhood memories but through blocks of childhood that are the becoming-child of the present.
—
Deleuze and Guattari, *What is Philosophy?*

These were my dreams for you and me, vieux copain—New Jews, the two of us, queer, militant, invisible, part of a possible new tribe bound by gossip and rumors of divine evidence.
—
Leonard Cohen, *Beautiful Losers*

TABLE OF CONTENTS

//hahaha//

/HhHhH///\\\hahaha//\/\\\AaAaA\\\///HhHhH///\\\
hahaha///\\\AaAaA\\\///HhHhH///\\\hahaha//\/\\
\AaAaA\\\///HhHhH///\\\hahaha///\\\AaAaA\\\///
HhHhH///\\\hahaha///\\\AaAaA\\\///HhHhH///\\\
hahaha///\\\AaAaA\\\///HhHhH///\\\hahaha///\\\
\AaAaA\\\///HhHhH///\\\hahaha//\/\\\AaAaA\\\///
HhHhH///\\\hahaha///\\\AaAaA\\\///HhHhH///\\\
hahaha///\\\AaAaA\\\///HhHhH///\\\hahaha///\\\
\AaAaA\\\///HhHhH///\\\hahaha//\/\\\AaAaA\\\///
HhHhH///\\\hahaha///\\\AaAaA\\\///HhHhH///\\\
hahaha///\\\AaAaA\\\///HhHhH///\\\hahaha///\\\
\AaAaA\\\///HhHhH///\\\hahaha//\/\\\AaAaA\\\///
HhHhH///\\\hahaha//\/\\\AaAaA\\\///HhHhH///\\\
hahaha///\\\AaAaA\\\///HhHhH///\\\hahaha//\/\\
\AaAaA\\\///HhHhH///\\\hahaha//\/\\\AaAaA\\\///
HhHhH///\\\hahaha///\\\AaAaA\\\///HhHhH///\\\
hahaha///\\\AaAaA\\\///HhHhH///\\\hahaha///\\\
\AaAaA\\\///HhHhH///\\\hahaha//\/\\\AaAaA\\\///
HhHhH///\\\hahaha///\\\AaAaA\\\///HhHhH///\\\
hahaha///\\\AaAaA\\\///HhHhH///\\\hahaha///\\\
\AaAaA\\\///HhHhH///\\\hahaha//\/\\\AaAaA\\\///
HhHhH///\\\hahaha///\\\AaAaA\\\///HhHhH///\\\
hahaha///\\\AaAaA\\\///HhHhH///\\\hahaha///\\\
\AaAaA\\\///HhHhH///\\\hahaha//\/\\\AaAaA\\\///
HhHhH///\\\hahaha///\\\AaAaA\\\///HhHhH///\\\
hahaha///\\\AaAaA\\\///HhHhH///\\\hahaha///\\\
\AaAaA\\\///HhHhH///\\\hahaha///\\\AaAaA\\\///
HhHhH///\\\hahaha///\\\AaAaA\\\///HhHhH///\\\
hahaha//\/\\\AaAaA\\\///HhHhH///\\\hahaha///\\\
\AaAaA\\\///HhHhH///\\\hahaha///\\\AaAaA\\\///
HhHhH///\\\hahaha//\/\\\AaAaA\\\///HhHhH///\\\
hahaha//\/\\\AaAaA\\\///HhHhH///\\\hahaha///\\\
\AaAaA\\\///HhHhH///\\\hahaha///\\\AaAaA\\\///
HhHhH///\\\hahaha///\\\AaAaA\\\///HhHhH///\\\
HhHhH///\\\hahaha///\\\AaAaA\\\///HhHhH///\\\
hahaha///\\\AaAaA\\\///HhHhH///\\\hahaha///\\\
\AaAaA\\\///HhHhH///\\\hahaha///\\\AaAaA\\\///
HhHhH///\\\hahaha//\/\\\AaAaA\\\///HhHhH///\\\
hahaha///\\\AaAaA\\\///HhHhH///\\\hahaha//\/\\

EXPOSED! MLA Chernoff Rothschild Deep State Neo-Marxist Protocols RARE FOOTAGE (2019)

Somebody once [hold] me
the world is gonna [hold] me—
please hold me.

I'm so hot for you I could melt steel beams.
In any and all cases, you're an asshole—
splay into my bidder sweets, sweaty;
there's no need to squelch it to me,
this slaying invocation, vocating me
wildly. Simply—

call me off
and awful my call.

delet this was published by
Bad Books
in the spring of 1991.

TERSE THIRSTY was published by
Gap Riot Press
in the spring of 1968.

But then:
      My two rabbis sub your Reddit
      and cosplay little ponies;
      a dialectic deeply stated,
      a Wall Street deep-keep nixed, unplaited.
Kill 'em with mine-ness, they say.
You can bet your bottom donner
they've hacked your bank account.
Neigh, they've elongated your musk
to a dearth of grimy Soundclouds;
means seized meanly—
no hard feelies to your inched-in
Heelys.

Shrieking in Shreks to orphan all the donkeys—
it's full-on rage, these
callus-round blouses
I sweat and pleather lightly.

3

Talk birdy to me and stand
thirty thousand plateaued paces
left of right so we can
shake in the sensuous: it's a living.
Are we not millennials?
We are DEVO.

In the end, it matters
if it's a pome or a praxis:
if the seas do seek a crop of cis with which
to drop a topple, just remember
my yawning yoni
and the code word
will appear.
CSIS is listening.
I'll kiss you
I'll miss you
I'll piss you
at the safe house.

In logic, you are tenses—
whence the hush of my septum,
splitting yes and no.
Oops!
Smelling in spells, I've lost my deposit.
It's the return of the repressed,
rimming 'round the posi.
Rocketful of—
have you tried exorcising?
Are you hydrated?

Sorry we didn't get a chance to talk at the show last night
I was super out of it and the profile you are trying to
view has been suspended because it goes against our
community guidelines.

to ripe and to not, not
squelching after Stein[1]

[Not] [Ripe]
There ain't no [not] [ripe] answer. There ain't gonna [not] be any [ripe] answer. There never [not] has been an answer so [ripe]. That's the [ripe] answer. Everybody gets so much [ripe] information all day long that they lose their [not] common [ripe] sense. Anything scares me, anything scares anyone [ripe] but really after all considering how dangerous everything is nothing is [not] really very frightening. It takes a lot of time to be a [ripe] genius, you have to sit around so much [not] doing nothing, really [not] doing nothing [ripe]. Generally speaking, [not] everyone is more interesting doing [not] nothing than [not] doing anything [ripe]. A writer should write [ripe] with [not] eyes and a painter [not] paint with [ripe] ears. Silent gratitude isn't [not] very much use to anyone [ripe].

[Not]
Collapsing freights instigate *mein sein*;
a rose is [not] a rose is [not] certainly a [not] rose—
composed in amicable getups attacking all exits;
later taking the eggs, being
insistent upon [not] dregs and
lippy singsongs. Cordially yours I am [not] now—
cordially in sores fasting in the daylight's break.
Of tremulous penny loafers mincing all floors
and the spaniel left drying in wrecked ice cream stores.
Nevertheless, tit for tit and tat for tat: Lizzie minds, Rose
    minds
all seven or eight of them goddamn mind but he
drives off to California. Yielding no stop signs, mirrors
    blurred
and dwindling, the pinked background—so very tired.
We: left delighted, [not] [not].
Disconcerting: willowed wisps without anchorage, steam
    and drizzle,
pillowing pillows. A piano plays its [not] in severance; the

---

1   https://www.google.com/search?q=gertrude+stein+quotes&rlz=1C5CHFA_enCA816CA816&oq=gertrude+stein+quotes&aqs=chrome..69i57j69i60j0l4.4010j0j4&sourceid=chrome&ie=UTF-8

    CRA bemoans
communal ties and woes:
the erasure's songstress still in her flight, of airborne ruts
    and tulip sights.

[Ripe]
I'm actually actually and that's factual
I'm actually quite angry at all times and that's
actual.
Was you hornier than me?
Probably not.
Two fidgets fig a freak of frolics &
it's like
oh.
So, trickle me fricken to do what is
⌐or what's wont. The lake is
hackling its own reflection,
retroflecting manicured manuals
for the foresight of a time-trapped
hob-bomber, a goop of predilections that
harken back to you, wooing.
Then—it's settled, empirical fricatives
snugging the snot of some piss-n-shit lover,
where, into the gardener's garden, we were where we were—
all the men have been collected into the vacuum
of eschatonic boondoggle,
viz. that knot-[ripe] fact of being wherein
we are [not] always the same [ripe] age inside.

Does My Assss Reveal Itself as the Horizon of Being?

⬛ordan ⬛eterson is just Heidegger for "incels."
The only good ⬤ Nazi is a 🅰🅰 dead ⬤⬤ Nazi—no shid!!!

These axioms should be
or are already
tautly taught 🔖
as 🅰🅰 tautology—
now *that's* the tightness of a
sweet, squelchy, dodgy, dogmatic
pedagogy.

For simplicity's shaky sake ⌣ ,
let's quadruple this line ⠀⠀⠀ of thought ⬤
in a 🅰 triple-time ⬤ brine
of ⸴ found ⸴ -grounded escape, 🆘 so 🆘 we can
gaggle their're slimed-up ⬜ , gaity masts
and rly just put a 🅰 sock in it𝛑!

I'm ANGRY:

A – about to jack ⬤ off ⬤
N – to
G – a 🅰 pome about myself
R – ⠀⠀ :')
Y – ⠀⠀⠀⠀⠀⠀⠀ ;') ⠀⠀⠀ hehehehehehehe

I would like 👫 that if you could
⚖ please ⚖
call 📱📱 me by your
... WAH
lest I ⬛ start ⬛⬛ to
... WAH

Angst? Oh, you 😋 mean 😋 Mondays
and who ordered 🍝 this fucking lasagna?
Not in MY counterculture!!!
There's only ☐ one ☐☐ gender ⬤
(GARFIELD).
NOUS SOMMES TOUS

DES JUIFS ALLEMANDS.
So, thus the French squelched
as structures both did and did not
walk the streets.

It all ✎ rings ✎ on ⇄ in repetitive traditions
of muttering a naught ⇄ on ⇄ a nothing.

Makin' and takin' all them
mighty demands as ▲ a ▲
jazzercise in utility.

I'm speaking ♟ cryptically
to prove the haters right ⬤.
Rightly in the wrong,
the speculative spectrum
of my other ass
is ▲ a ▲ ♣ club ♣ kid candied with tabernacles,
knuckling forth into foam roaming
trenched-up ▲ ▲ ♈ ceremonies ♈ of
becoming-Party Munster
and other ⚘ spicy ⚘ pronouns.

I'm just a ▲ poet and lief is a ▲ nightmare.
I'm just the space ̆ between the /o/ and the /e/:
Here are my desires.

SQUELCH i (Mercury in Paris)

The Simple Life (2003-2005)
is an intrusive memory of the future—
a squelch shared by all, goading psalm-gobbed etches
onto the underside of rare Pogs I bog into
swole-ass cymose, next to the squelch
I find under
the couch
during a c r y i n g spell about the metaphysics
of mommy and other ontic antics in
a well-mannered Bathurst of familiar fun:
here's to the joy, all m'sweet goys!

At the clean-shaven seder, I singe for a
type-token cache to adequately analyze
Frank Sinatra and his
snot-poshed knavery
while his pall-mall voice
projects itself in and around
the jeers of astral wax nuggets I call ear—

                                        damn.

It's a sorry night for 23andMe;
according to my therapist,
my true family is true,
my true family, truly;
the stars in the night sky are
my true family, like a frown touted
by the squelch of one helix
hugging its other.

Squelch is that feeling when
your only family heirloom is being
lost in a Walmart full of shit-rusted
Norman Doors, where us poors
go for the privacy but stay for the Rollbacked™
sense of sylph. But here's the sitch: I am that I am—
a race car grin, a Trotsky-assed guilt complex:
that's hot.

Simply footed, squelch lobs me into
a circus of circuits, seduces seduction
and inverts its induction, heating me
with another possible possible;
cracking out a cold Sidekick,
I take down its number,
place bets on its gematria and
kiss my next of kin, for whom I
am always amiss.

Squelch imbibes so many
forgive-me-nots—missives of bliss and cherry rots,
such-that-the wheelchair's funk endlessly childs
all my little husks and paints little alien babies,
spilling the uncharitable lightness of tomato soup
all over my goddamn Being. Squelch imbibes until I

turn down the volume.

Later-still I dunk my comrade, my opulence—
her name is Sailor Mercury
and I dunk her into the bowl and I
drink of her; I become her, into the bowl I go,
for a quick swirl
into the bowl, pipe-hot and chafing for a tuck,
if only for a lip-exonerated blip—
you shout at me. But why?
It's canon, it's retrograde.
I stain the plush chair in all
its cinnabar glory; I walk away
Assigned Measles At Birth,
my toes in my snout, spitting up Gryfe's (3421 Bathurst St.),
attempting to access the grief and peel back the anger,
a banana, barking of forgone skin, returning to envelope me.
> A splinter kisses my foot through our shit-brown carpet and I
> weep into eternity, if only for a moment, tucking the chafe away.

Then and there, squelch lurches into me,
pinging my spleen by the beeper.
For $1100 a month, it rents the space between
idealism and ideation, where procedure is as moot as the
        balcony
I find myself thrusting toward, over and under gauche-
        green
curtains, miles away from your volume
and the guck of your bathroom where clipped fingernails
        ween
hot compresses into a macabre dance of comedogenics,
fucking genetics in the key of acne-free eugenics,
sitting without shitting for hours on end and
twiddling my bums around the memory
of a cockroach greeting my wetness with the
hiss of a decorative towel, damp with
magmatic miasmas who down issues
of *Women's World* and suck the stream of
non- in a good binch's conscience.
In short, the squelch of old hat and old house—
a never-knot in remission—founds my body on the
tenderness of a too-hot-4-u spleen pouring bisque,
                              misdelivered.

13

```
///HhHhH///\\\hahaha///\\\\AaAaA\\\///HhHhH///\\
\hahaha///\\\\AaAaA\\\///HhHhH///\\\hahaha///\\\
\AaAaA\\\///HhHhH///\\\hahaha///\\\\AaAaA\\\///H
hHhH///\\\hahaha///\\\\AaAaA\\\///HhHhH///\\\ha
haha///\\\\AaAaA\\\///HhHhH///\\\hahaha///\\\\Aa
AaA\\\///HhHhH///\\\hahaha///\\\\AaAaA\\\///HhH
hH///\\\hahaha///\\\\AaAaA\\\///HhHhH///\\\haha
ha///\\\\AaAaA\\\///HhHhH///\\\hahaha///\\\\AaAa
A\\\///HhHhH///\\\hahaha///\\\\AaAaA\\\///HhHhH
///\\\hahaha///\\\\AaAaA\\\///HhHhH///\\\hahaha/
//\\\\AaAaA\\\///HhHhH///\\\hahaha///\\\\AaAaA\\\
///HhHhH///\\\hahaha///\\\\AaAaA\\\///HhHhH///\\
\hahaha///\\\\AaAaA\\\///HhHhH///\\\hahaha///\\\
\AaAaA\\\///HhHhH///\\\hahaha///\\\\AaAaA\\\///H
hHhH///\\\hahaha///\\\\AaAaA\\\///HhHhH///\\\ha
haha///\\\\AaAaA\\\///HhHhH///\\\hahaha///\\\\Aa
AaA\\\///HhHhH///\\\hahaha///\\\\AaAaA\\\///HhH
hH///\\\hahaha///\\\\AaAaA\\\///HhHhH///\\\haha
ha///\\\\AaAaA\\\///HhHhH///\\\hahaha///\\\\AaAa
A\\\///HhHhH///\\\hahaha///\\\\AaAaA\\\///HhHhH
///\\\hahaha///\\\\AaAaA\\\///HhHhH///\\\hahaha/
//\\\\AaAaA\\\///HhHhH///\\\hahaha///\\\\AaAaA\\\
///HhHhH///\\\hahaha///\\\\AaAaA\\\///HhHhH///\\
\hahaha///\\\\AaAaA\\\///HhHhH///\\\hahaha///\\\
\AaAaA\\\///HhHhH///\\\hahaha///\\\\AaAaA\\\///H
hHhH///\\\hahaha///\\\\AaAaA\\\///HhHhH///\\\ha
haha///\\\\AaAaA\\\///HhHhH///\\\hahaha///\\\\Aa
AaA\\\///HhHhH///\\\hahaha///\\\\AaAaA\\\///HhH
hH///\\\hahaha///\\\\AaAaA\\\///HhHhH///\\\haha
ha///\\\\AaAaA\\\///HhHhH///\\\hahaha///\\\\AaAa
A\\\///HhHhH///\\\hahaha///\\\\AaAaA\\\///HhHhH
///\\\hahaha///\\\\AaAaA\\\///HhHhH///\\\hahaha/
//\\\\AaAaA\\\///HhHhH///\\\hahaha///\\\\AaAaA\\\
///HhHhH///\\\hahaha///\\\\AaAaA\\\///HhHhH///\\
\AaAaA\\\///HhHhH///\\\hahaha///\\\\AaAaA\\\///H
hHhH///\\\hahaha///\\\\AaAaA\\\///HhHhH///\\\ha
haha///\\\\AaAaA\\\///HhHhH///\\\hahaha///\\\\Aa
AaA\\\///HhHhH///\\\hahaha///\\\\AaAaA\\\///HhH
hH///\\\hahaha///\\\\AaAaA\\\///HhHhH///\\\haha
ha///\\\\AaAaA\\\///HhHhH///\\\hahaha///\\\\AaAa
A\\\///HhHhH///\\\hahaha///\\\\AaAaA\\\///HhHhH
```

Digression I: Baba Yaga Kills a Holocaust Denier (Battery Park, NYC)

Finally! Some rest and relaxation.

How to Kiss Like a Spinozist

Oh, enema of the skin—
there is only one pome in this collection,
and it is this one:
        a cross-legged inkblot
swaying on command,
triangulating $40 facial serum
into the langue of a
busy training day, learning
to oust a cop to deadland with
glistening brow and heavy-handed knuckleballing,
the kind of Molotov you wouldn't
kiss your dermatologist with.

You're scratching up a
funky, funky mix of:
yes! We really do exist, we come from
sun dust and hashtags left clothe-pinned
in blime-nosing winter, where the noise
won't cancel itself with nuance-blocking
butt plugs, blunt-shy of metaphor, lolling
into the meridian of a flaming
squad car.[1]

Simply and overtly,
you make your parents proud,
but I'm just as loud.
I ask of you to polish my lens,
over and over again.

Pink my affordances with
a ray of the spray,
let me dash the day away
in bed-bread and yeast-head.
Listen, I need you to yeet this my way:
        a pome not simply
        about depression;
        a pome that is
        depression itself,

---

1   https://www.youtube.com/watch?v=gVwLqEHDCQE

a pome that sees me,
and feels the way the body
can monetize itself in the
final analysis of
$141.25 per session, per capita.

Accessing grief and peeling back the anger;
a foreskin regrowing itself in the tic of a
sad sappy day!
Rain? Ohhhhhhh, mommy no!

In affordance of this frankhood,
I must sashay unto you.
Like a truth becoming truth,
scrunching in affordances—
a tax paying itself over
in duplicitous debt and horny matrimony,
paring our parents' salaries,
salivating cuts whose names
are windswept and forever kept.

Sashay, sashay them all—all of your fucks
away. It's 2019 you bet you oughta
second-to-none that
time-trapped metronome of an ass
a.k.a. the metrophobic slur hurled
at you on the subway
that awakened your old longing
for the new, new, new (I got a lot).

This portrait of your shoes—
traversing unfamiliar terrain—
is encrypted with a cutting red tape
and roping red flags full of mythic fire;
the predations of Fordism and
social devastation,
heretofore a post-Fordism in and as the
bloody tarmac bluing out the

sedan, economic euphoria that
sanctions a society within society;
we live in a society
on a planetary scale, on a podium
of razors (the best)
the image of prophesy (a man can get)
from the Stoic to the makeshift arts fund
it took to publish selfhood—
does Pagliacci even eat ass?

Eateries and eternities
of shit, shan't, and shunned.
Memories of spring, spraining my
sprung. Who is third? The third?
Unicorn or otherwise?
I am not myself until I call myself
on a dusty old landline:
Je est un otter
(reads RAMBO once).

In conclusion,
affections and predilections
don't fuck around;
they don't enlighten
the bug-red night of a middlebound
torso, in brine and lean,
insisting you
awaken the sweet sheet
as son and as child,
testifying titular,
spaying testaments to
squeamishness:
bold and mutable are
those gorgemouth buffoons
pillowing the death bed.

Though shaken, you'll
let it dawn on you,
like mustard in the mild.

That the odds are getting good—
　　　this is no lie.
The odds are getting good.

When false friends pucker up
to translate the desk,
conditionals spew out
stewy premises.
Break-necks drip anaphora
from the edge of showerheads
into the hole of a night
unveiling.

While stowaways rest
upon foaméd tress,
chortling worlds gnash themselves
between elbows and marshed-out mellows
that brink and maim,
engulfing aspects of grief:
loves that once loved
and losses that once lost.
Yes, it's like that:
　　　ole-timey pish-posh.

Belatedly, I ask you to
take each pore, and fill it with each pore:
Death is a tooth among strangers,
upended by dentists and ontologists every which where.
Listen, my delicious GreekJew:
I don't mean to sound logocentric,
but words are facialized fossils,
skying the page with another
pome about pomes,
ampersands about ampersands—
they are true
like truth,
like true truths that you
ain't never heard before.

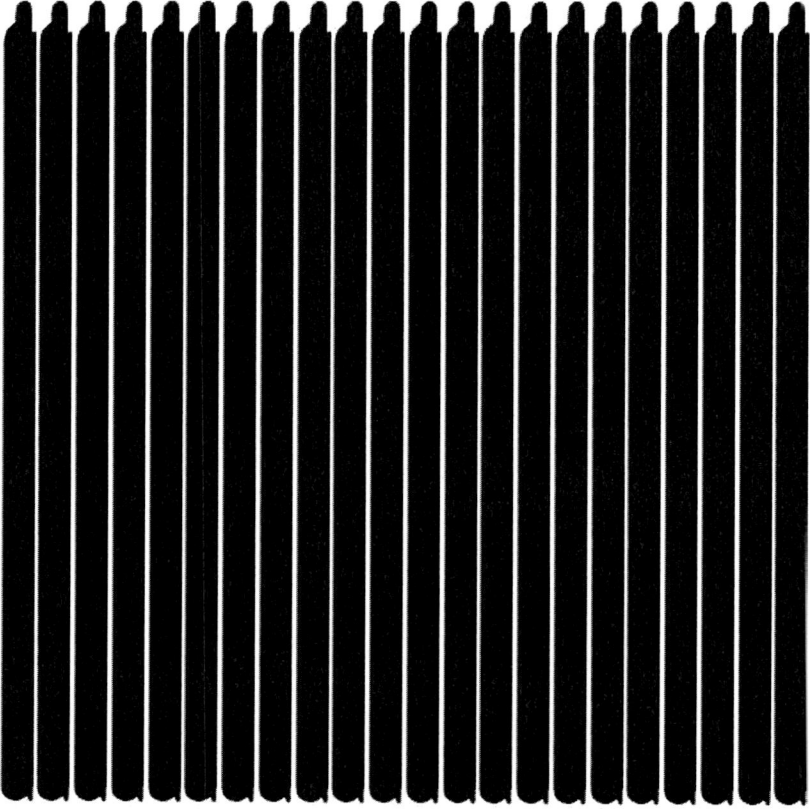

Welcome to the Lawrence Plaza;
we've really got it all. I am a Toronto price,
enticing *frumas* to child wigged propensities.
I love the family, but I worry that they lack
oedipality—oy vey.

I am the family, a triangle of
filth—you can have it all,
my empire of GIRTH.

GET READY!

5
-
4
-
3
-
2
-
1
-
-
-
-
-

I'll be right back.

I'm taking the wind tunnel to the temple
where I've been trying to excommunicate
my own ass
from the 14th floor of its *venti* boudoir.

Polishing—rag to lens, cumming up
with blurred nonce rambles and a
bucket of piss.

Mind to mind: all my friends are
syllogistic singers surging
through affirmation,
and surely, I'll be more
choosing than chosen:
my friends over you,
maybe a shawarma or two;
let's laugh in all the laffas
today.

In Bathurst I'm a manner,
but no language will Christ me out of
chewy contemplation.
No me is neutral.

No language is me.
There was a Dionne Brand reference in there
somewhere. You should probably just
read her
instead.

Do not wait for me while
I stretch this street through space
and time—I'm death, I'm the
critic no one asked for,
a manor without light or fight.

Flight belongs to no one.
Not even the rain
can stay on brand.
Nor a snowball, nor a
dragonfly could harden my ware
at the park, in shot or shimmer.

In any case,
it's truly a fable from which
we could tickle back our eyes
into the lack of sheds we shed,
where the outside looms through
the absence of caulking and
shuttered-in beginnings bone out bugs listlessly
into endings that duddle psalms for palms,
as pilots dry-up in sweaty peachdom,
kindly marring the night into a martyrdom
surmised by crystals.
I've only
cans of abundance
filled to the grim with
self-striking matchsticks.

I bite the thicket of a dusk sweeping
crust from wrinkle;
warm-wet sheets,
who unremember that
anaphora is merely friendship
in falsity, a game without favour:
       kissed by economy,
       and lobbing never-forevers,
       again and ago,
       until we rest, finally,
       in fugue and in forest
       and then, later,
       in snow.

Goo Goo Is Free, Sweaty (Squelched Kaddish)

Glorified and sanctified be
my great G-dly deadname
throughout the world which They has created
according to Their will.
May daddy Ginsberg establish a crass,
brassy wing-ding kingdom, somewhere in Florida,
of cancelled fuckos who are also sad
about their moms and we will all say,
I hate all men—amen.

In your lifetime and during your days,
and within the virtuality of all
the foot pics I never shook
nor took in the house of
that Israeli boy who should,
with rigour-vigour,
go fuck himself,
I do wish that thou wouldst
speedily and soon spay those words and say,
I hate all men—amen.

May the rabbi's son forever want my coke—
in suspension and expulsion, a diarrheal realty
of a peeled pencil choke, exuding realities,
glorified, exalted, extolled
on some New Jersey turnpike,
as long and schlongéd as Bathurst Street,
where I honour my ass
by shitting one out and spraying, together:
I hate all men—amen.

Adored and lauded be the
mane of that Holy Horse,
that one from *The Sopranos*
that Tony really liked, beyond all the
blessings, praises, and consultations that
are ever spoken in the world because I missed my
appointment again; and we shall say,
I hate all men—amen.

May there be abundant peace from heaven, and life, for us
and for all Palestine; and say, I hate all men—amen.
They who gets a vasectomy is actually just me
and please stop misgendering me and my
celestial thighs, where I create peace for myself.
Goo goo is free, sweaty, and you will,
I am for certain, Venmo me your true love and say,
I hate all men—amen.

a piping hot bowl of chills
friendo-ship squelch 4 bill bissett on his 80th brethday

When you fed me those first chills, I flubbed:
what fuckan lunch?
more of a pome bespoken in the clarity of charities—
three-hundred flowers, dancing Lunarian,
potted in the early early where the glaze flicks praise
through patio doors into everydayness,
rattling candelabras
misting toward pouched-in hat-heads and cloudy,
stuffed-about 8-tracks in pip-pip-pip paintings
who pant hyperspeed through so many
spines—the new breth, oohing and ahhing
in pastel and piccolo, where riverside vertebrates
swoon in so many woos of wistful wishes,
feeding forth fluxed-up feet with
little tiny itty bitty
piranha kisses:
no tongue, all toes, all cartilage—melting;
over fireside crucibles, rivering the recipe
with green, maybe aquamarine, margarine, and...
O! There you go—
        stirring red hot heat-things
            into the chills
              —excellent!
        morphing cluck-a-bucks
            into the chills
              —copy that!
        whirring weened clobber-snares
            into the chills
              —that's so hype!
        coring wing-ding ranch bots
            into the chills
              —wowee zowee!
        blobbing other bund fun-havers
            into the chills
              —oh dang, lmao!
[squelching] spices, face-first, into bowled love,
knighting rung after rung with another
set of lungs, pumping out jojoba oil
to praise the palms of psalm bombers,
of taste and of bud, fluttering about for future therapies

in warm hug embrace:—a shoe clack
stomping riverside, splaying pavement where
College becomes Carlton becomes dithyrambs
of burnt banknotes, hummed voluminous
for sweet November in the sizzle-blown mulch of
billions of tons of love letters sent to and fro
Mattawa, Uhauling themselves
into echoes of villages and rumours of
winter, meowing into the mouth of what?
Uh, hmmmm, henlo, friendo!—
a zonking reticular *excellence*; or,
just another way of
licking n linging sum langue
into the chills.

Digression II: Three Steps on The Ladder of Radicalizing Your Depression

I forgot to tell my therapist,
but I'm telling you:
in recent dreams, my cis-ass nephew,
mimesis, and a
deck of tarot cards
walk into a bar.

Yet again, once and again,
so it goes and it flows—a
transcendental ego
falling from my ass
in bird-like necrose,
slinking down the steps
of my walk-up
to take off the pant
and get into sweater:
it's weather for puppies
and it's belling a getter.

It isn't so much a joke as it is
a means for me to poke
and to poke
and to poke
and to poke
and to poke
and to poke
and to poke
and to poke
~~and to pick~~
my sour skin,
pore by gingko'd pore,
the fuck of remembrance
in things tossed and
salads uncrossed.

In experience, I'm exalted by ex-centricity.
Epistemologies may my day,
and, through exhortation,
evacuate my gift shop to
call my mother loudly:

are you alone?
Dream, baby, dream.
Outside with the cuties,
nightclubbing we sneeze.

My bank, you see, pours pores
by the bucket load,
staging anonymity by the fuck-it-load,
toading real-life fight clubs
in the garage with a
sabretooth light and a
song undone by its leather (whoa, whoa).

If the sacred is only ever profane,
then I have come here to tell you
all about all the pain and pro-pain accessories
in the plastic ramekin
of my takeout container.

When lovers converse,
they do not make demands:
        I am in lust with you and
        together we qualify for this Groupon.
        An offer of refuse, where we
        blow our noses
        aggressively
        to perfect the
        date night snack
        of our dreams;
        a Chalet sauce enema—
        no hair off my slacks.

As a friend, I syllogize you
to condition our conscience consumptively.
When a disordered excoriation meets
the chaos of our emptied excelsior,
everyone's tired
in the end.

Spay it, Seal: "WAH-WAH-WAH."
Spell it, Dolphin: "E-E-E-E-E."
Spray it—like rosewater toner
from the blowhole of your bottle
to the bottom of my mouth,
where the frolics are best
pulled shut of their Nestle-
nestled scales.

Repetition is what self-plagiarism
exclaims when a wound
seals itself shut, exploding
the old molecular
into the red dust of being—
or something.

The fuzz of my face
tells me to debate them,
to open future oddities
unto them.

But really,
I say:
       1.   1) Arm yourselves
            a.   a)   I'm scared
                   i. i)   Are you scared, too?

There's mace in the mail;
in its prime, an Amazon—
just another case of the
faster's tools frosting
my stench—
oh, the shame I claim
when I manage all potentials
to put you in my pudding.

My only kink is making weak the strong,
fashioning fists to blink them asunder,
fists and fits to pull me under sweat-wet sheets
where belonging thrums of homonyms
in yucky-sweet sorrows
that've lost their footing.

If only one could
transubstantiate
suicidal ideation
into
political assassination—
an alchemy of swooning remembrance
that mines itself free of the
canary's squawk-to-flee
those dialed-up
mow-slow policies.

Instead, I maybe just perhaps will
duplicate a duppy simcha
and prune these pungencies to
the undersides of Endys, where
mommy hoards her toonies and a few
pamphlets on squeezing the meekness
right out of your alimony using only
protestant chits of self-flagellation.

It's time to rouse my rash and
toss my cobbéd brain-for-shit
onto a plane of
infinite resignation,
one I have dug upward
for myself in the final analysis,
the last instance of cis,
designed by Sein,
a hoist of mows that meow
"so fuckan what?"

I come to you lurking from the depths
of a love named Sadie,
of a thou that therefore I am,
a non-equivalency
screeching of stonks and start-ups.

The synchronicity of $40
is the way it flaps erotically
through finger-fraught tusks
of windswept timebombs, tick-ticking.

It's a cheque that's checking in
and cashing out
on my abandonment issues,
offering a monied tissue
as though to agree that
the mother only mutters:
let the mother mutter or
make amends in butter—
you must practice only care.

I transubstantiate my care, but mostly,
I place my care in Elijah's chair,
I circumscribe my transubstantiated care
and continue to glare.

I'm an unborn again—alive and lovin' it.
The first time I became a coming
it reigned in a de-settled glint of propriety,
forming the foam of essentials.

A litre of chugged-about chuckles hail marrying
personal property into the
twilight of idyllic zones.

That is to say,
a reading lamp of one's own,
a place to fart very loudly,
veering toward a tarried rim, a round rosary
with the words "cop killer" inscribed
on its tailbone.

And I'm just starting to sense it,
jostling its rubbish, tongue-flat and helpless:
our sugary secret, our spice of
everything nice. No need for mezuzahs
where I'm going, no, not at all.

Outside the bed is the facticity of
of every bearded embargo I call follicle.
If there is nothing but after after,
I've found myself safe, at least,
in this ontological necessity: a lever
that can pull itself,
a dermatillomania
without flounder,
without thought—
a political theology
without anything about Schmitt
or his bullshit—
a carping pome, floating in piss,
lurching toward so many deities whose
regrets are later liquidated into
the profane thwacks
of a ball bouncing its inflation,
at noon and under the sun
in someone else's memory
of a nice, quiet day in the muscles
of a crystal-clear beach.

How Do You Spell S-Q-U-E-L-C-H?

That feeling when, there you are
       another Kafka, a spinning Lispector
in your fight-tight leotard, siphoning svelte and
marauding some hatchet down a thousand
winded kisses.

How do you spell squelch?
How do you spell any one thing
at this pissy point of
absolute departure, where
your grimacing ass in its grand biologism
puckers another plain goodbye?
"Good grief!!" it murmurs,
ad infinitum, aiming itself
at the chad Leninist leaflet
whose theorygram memes are so
based and pog-pilled, you would die
for them in a Hardtbeat.

How do you smell squelch?
You respond with a statement,
"Mimesis ain't (nothing but) shit,"
an argument which
ought to beg the question:
what is mimesis and
how can a meme be cis?

If writing is a missive on missing!
       ALLCAPS
If writing is a missive on kissing!
       ALLCAPS
Then writing
       ALLCAPS

ain't nothing but a
biomechanical war-torn bore,
a salt mine sex drive
slumming its gears in
slimy tedium, quartering its
Q's and H's, rendering them
a Presley'd star of comic fixtures
in a mild-mannered critique
of the prison industrial complex.
        In the totalizing funked-to-death swell of your well,
        it seems that you have successfully spelled it:
                shuelcq, baby, shuelcq

ONE MORE FINAL: I need you (Neoliberal Squelch by MLA Chernoff)

My arms squelch on for centuries, erasing the Hebrew calendar and grousing grips into the solitude of discursive strategies—invoiced meadows billowing at the sea of things in all its gory glory.

I've always never been—just kidding, who am I to say what a depressive episode is or could be. I love you, please pilot the Eva for me, lest I lay waste to a brand-new pair of Fentys that fit only me. 400% Synchronization.

Oops the edible has kicked in. The oops has oopsed along sideways into the rectal cavity of a body I've unimagined to the point of HEADLINES. There is sufficiency in saying this—my Chiron is in Leo, my Chiron is cacophonous—synchrony sexting diachrony's cronies. I fasten my haste to the back of a listicle on finally learning to live, finally. What, then, is the difference?

Yadda yadda yadda: repetition, push-pin plexities mounting essential oils. I know you exist, I knead you, where are you. And I'm so sorry. It's a curious incident of a sweater in the night whereupon I breast my head to maim the mattress and cough myself to breath, as though I'd—hitherto, too—never heard myself hearing.

Don't ya know I've always been this way? A trench coat full of slotted machine plagiarizers whose metaphysics breakfast upon the love love love I sicken to unsee in a so-called heterosexuality. This is the part my therapist applauds in the language of laryngitis, so I know that love can be more than muffled transferences.

Here are my particularities: a parent to my age, twenty-six and a half, balding at the toe and gunking out my jelly as though a clipper hadn't kissed my years in decades. I've seen it all, a dome-to-ball known-it-all that's travelled from here to nowhere and back again.

Yes, that's right: my ass, my crack, my gumption, and my frack. I turn up the heat and splay a toonie out of my churned-over stomach in the form of: give me veganism or give me death. One time I took a shit and it looked like Vegandale: it was Vegandale, it was Wilmington Plaza.

There's a deathly death that drives the one hundred million billion corporations who've saged six thousand billion trillion years off the stickéd end of a buttercup fork: we call it the subject swimming, edging lords off the flat, flat earth.

In conclusion, Grinchhood is *bashert*—it's an Eva well-piloted, rearing its own damn socks andor sandals to the armoury, stealing extinction under the cork-tide of posterity and other fine wares. There, I said it—there.

Theorems on the Good News by François Laruelle by MLA Chernoff

<u>Theorem 0; or, the Transcendental Theorem,</u>
<u>On Non-transferable Identity</u>

Eros is the stink of all verbs,
bound to some faraway
beach where
half-lives kiss the half-light
      of jilted sentiments
& bisected coconuts bear
the weight of their own
snared semblances:
a fridge well lit,
made crisp
by harm, by amour.

Ouef.

It is neither:
metaphor   nor   metonymy.
                thus
[T]here [can be] no
      reversibility.

Theorem 00—On the Statute

Thanatos is my butt
slamming against your butt,
growing enormous and vibratory.
[I]nnumerable
                    and solitary [...]
obtained before any kind of identification.

Death plants
the thickness of its absence
in the skull of
my butt.

Those who pretend to
[squelch] God and the Subject [...]
are disabused by [this] announcement.

Theorem 000—On the Abolition of the Statute

Each time I leave my laptop unattended
at the library, I bequeath to passersby
a message on an otherwise blank Word document.
"Stealing this computer won't explain poetry"—
a lie emboldened, size 36 Papyrus.

[The] impotence of thought [is its]
infinite culpability: [a]n event
without remainder, a generic whatever,
a who we must woo.
It is the way we endlessly circumscribe
the contours of our plumped and pompous faces,
asking, "when did you become so various?"

U and I:
the difference between sully and silly.
You and I:
jesting gestation, arms engulfing legs—a oneness so frilly.

[T]he announcement is identical to the Abolition of the
    Statute.
The announcement announces nothing if not itself.
It is an old Jewish joke the colour of smoke;
it is three Minion™ emoji, rubbing my coke.

[P]hilosophy, then, is already made,
but made for [squelch]
and for [squelch]
to rejoice in beholding it and it
beholding [squelch]—:
palliatively pressing its
twos into ones, meats out of buns,
muffling all its little Maoisms
back into their great big tank,
where they can be hospitalized for
approaching perfection.

[P]hilosophy, then, is already made,
it is a sigh, reeking: "O.K."
It is the way your lovence may teem with the stupor
of its own ream (emboldened, size 36 Papyrus, and
breathy at the seams).

23andMe (starry night)

[   ]

Fatherhood and motherhood are always
a compromise between a form of Nazi eugenics
and a compulsion for repetition.
—Paul B. Preciado

According to my therapist,
the stars in the night sky are my true family.
It's this velvet flood of metaphor
by which I relish in all things,
both keeping and kept—
in and of extinction, a sixth time 'round
the fountain, reeling in exactitude
because it's the seventh time
I've lost your hairbrush to
a puckering petri dish.

Oh, this cruciferous clump of ass hair,
it's all so abrupt, the way it clogs
the stinked up sink of fertile ailments,
the way I pick and fuddle pores
to cloister clubbing nerves by salicylic masonry,
those iambic whims of witcheries that
say *no more* no more.

4am Squelch (Building Most Secret Hidden Underground Tunnel House By Ancient Skills In Deep Jungle TIMELAPSE)

To survey and surtitle a surrebuttal at dawn,
it drools in surveille a blue-light surrey,
glow-going a miser sure-footed in thingness,

        surecasting a surf in surjective surrender,
      flinging surreptitiousness, a Chrome-blasted
        sojourn toward a sheet-worn worry

in time to surtax each photo and each app
in on surrogate space where it
surveys survival and gives to enrich each

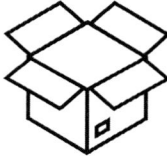

other's arrival and to dig and surprise and
surround in surmise, to pluck and to beg
in surcharges and rent in moats of surcoats

where surfaces do bloat to surge in its surgeon
to fish in the night where a
spurge dawns a mullet in all surplus'd delight.

Oh! all in due time, a
Breton for Bataille in surrejoinder, in eye,
a baton for a lie with which to untie
this truncheon, to wait, a tree sprouting
goodbye and
oops—I'm too

Great job! But be careful: Fire + no oxygen / ventilation = go to sleep and never wake up again How many tools have these people gone through.....

These people would most likely survive the apocalypse if it ever happens.....I love the creativity behind all this these vids make me want to get to work crafting and making with my own hands! Bro i want them to

make a series on making a full village or something. i hope they're getting paid for this or taken care of at least They make beautifull rooms underground, but they wont last very long. The first thing when it rain it will flooded by water and mud. Maybe they can build a underground design which will last longer, maybe long enough to do another video of surviving in the jungle

SQUELCH ii (Warbles for Wellbutrin)

Nothing knows no one more than me;
the pome is the beauty of this—
the way my hairline squares away at my
hairline, plagiarizing velvet-eared
Purim costumes to quarantine
the overflow of vines and timelines as
a hamantash swamps the last madeleine crumb
and pays me off in a wide-awake
desert of the feels, demanding sleep
and other masks—squelching.

Each strand is an oily discourse spewing nonce,
triangulating from head to fore and all the way to floor,
      where
it becomes quite clear that the dandruff is the damage done.
But let's be honest—the "D" in C-PTSD stands for
diaper if you're as nervous as my
stomach is Jewish, if you're as white as my ass is humid.

Notwithstanding, squelch is brine-tingled,
a greeting that lowballs its geometry in the backlot
of a used-car emporium, tucking away its mileage: oh,
daddy, daddy.
Twenty odd years and I'm as
bourgeois as a brioche in the midday sun,
chatting up my intrusive thoughts as quickly as a
a dent-can of Ensure enters me with
the sureness of your gratitudes, replying-all
to every under-slept email with a
hope this finds you well
when really, it's just a matter of
I'll see you tenured TERFs in hell.
I bcc that sweet spot, where the sphincter meets the root
chakra
and kisses are signed to unemployment cheques therein:
nourishment.

In reality, it's 13 going on 5779 and my face really reels it;
that feeling when histories of herstories become theirstories
and my bones cake apart my bones, accordingly.
But really, my vocabulary did this to me.
Pomes are "always already" CBD-infused,
clung out in the genders of my ownmost sylph,
an 8th wonder I nick in the nick of time.
It's enough to leave the frums looking askance at the load—
that's so sad:

> Alexa, play *dai-dai-yenu* and kiss
> that dead toad.

///HhHhH///\\\hahaha//\\\AaAaA\\\///HhHhH//\\
\hahaha///\\\AaAaA\\\///HhHhH///\\\hahaha//\\\
\AaAaA\\\///HhHhH//\\\hahaha///\\\AaAaA\\\///H
hHhH///\\\hahaha//\\\AaAaA\\\///HhHhH//\\\ha
haha//\\\AaAaA\\\///HhHhH///\\\hahaha//\\\Aa
AaA\\\///HhHhH///\\\hahaha///\\\AaAaA\\\///HhH
hH///\\\hahaha///\\\AaAaA\\\///HhHhH///\\\haha
ha//\\\AaAaA\\\///HhHhH///\\\hahaha//\\\AaAa
A\\\///HhHhH///\\\hahaha///\\\AaAaA\\\///HhHhH
//\\\hahaha//\\\AaAaA\\\///HhHhH//\\\hahaha/
//\\\AaAaA\\\///HhHhH//\\\hahaha//\\\AaAaA\\\
///HhHhH///\\\hahaha//\\\AaAaA\\\///HhHhH//\\
\hahaha///\\\AaAaA\\\///HhHhH//\\\hahaha//\\\
\AaAaA\\\///HhHhH//\\\hahaha//\\\AaAaA\\\///H
hHhH//\\\hahaha//\\\AaAaA\\\///HhHhH//\\\ha
haha//\\\AaAaA\\\///HhHhH//\\\hahaha//\\\Aa
AaA\\\///HhHhH///\\\hahaha///\\\AaAaA\\\///HhH
hH///\\\hahaha//\\\AaAaA\\\///HhHhH//\\\haha
ha///\\\AaAaA\\\///HhHhH//\\\hahaha//\\\AaAa
A\\\///HhHhH///\\\hahaha//\\\AaAaA\\\///HhHhH
//\\\hahaha///\\\AaAaA\\\///HhHhH///\\\hahaha
//\\\AaAaA\\\///HhHhH///\\\hahaha//\\\AaAaA\\\
///HhHhH//\\\hahaha//\\\AaAaA\\\///HhHhH//\\
\hahaha///\\\AaAaA\\\///HhHhH//\\\hahaha///\\
\AaAaA\\\///HhHhH//\\\hahaha//\\\AaAaA\\\///H
hHhH///\\\hahaha//\\\AaAaA\\\///HhHhH//\\\ha
haha///\\\AaAaA\\\///HhHhH//\\\hahaha//\\\Aa
AaA\\\///HhHhH///\\\hahaha///\\\AaAaA\\\///HhH
hH///\\\hahaha///\\\AaAaA\\\///HhHhH//\\\haha
ha//\\\AaAaA\\\///HhHhH//\\\hahaha//\\\AaAa
A\\\///HhHhH///\\\hahaha///\\\AaAaA\\\///HhHhH
//\\\hahaha///\\\AaAaA\\\///HhHhH//\\\hahaha/
/\\\AaAaA\\\///HhHhH//\\\hahaha//\\\AaAaA\\\
///HhHhH//\\\hahaha//\\\AaAaA\\\///HhHhH//\\
\hahaha///\\\AaAaA\\\///HhHhH//\\\hahaha//\\\
\AaAaA\\\///HhHhH//\\\hahaha//\\\AaAaA\\\///H
hHhH///\\\hahaha///\\\AaAaA\\\///HhHhH//\\\ha
haha///\\\AaAaA\\\///HhHhH//\\\hahaha//\\\Aa
AaA\\\///HhHhH///\\\hahaha///\\\AaAaA\\\///HhH
hH///\\\hahaha///\\\AaAaA\\\///HhHhH//\\\haha
ha///\\\AaAaA\\\///HhHhH//\\\hahaha//\\\AaAa
A\\\///HhHhH///\\\hahaha//\\\AaAaA\\\///HhHhH

Waluigi is Non-Binary and I Will Die on this Hill

Biologically, I am forty milligrams of Citalopram,
aching dust onto the subway floor.
You reach out to cough my throat,
I sink in the deep sweater, the tunnel-hugged
walls stained with clout-green amnesties and
consumer bouts—pouting, tongues wide and out.

I have many many-gendered-mothers,
none of whom I can seemly sway my day with,
all of whom are quotes for whom I list my lists,
counting sheep in proximity to that eye
begotten Eye—m'taskmaster!
Oh, sweet and sweaty and salty Eye—
do you have no story?
Why yes, m'theydy, you spry themperor.
Oh, fuck it—I'm sleepy, just call me a slur.

OK, I'm back to the old pomes:
lmao haha lol roflcopter.
Just kidding. It's true, I'm distracted by this pathos,
it's no mythos that my hand-cold cellular is its own logos
posting cringe on a global scale,
drowning the old Transatlanticisms,
in puddles of negation and brash centrisms,
pointing in all directions and scratching up the tarmac
with bite-away nails and pouting red flames,
WAH-ing itself awake in the middle of its blame.

[Squelching] a Coke with Y;ou

is either more or less Pinteresting than drying out my
    sobriety
in the haze of a loan-hungry *vaporwave*—
toking in the chops and the screws as if thou wert
the whole dang world,
by myself; alone at night; lonelysad,
fucked—both boujee and bad.

Doing Pepsi—just one Pepsi—with you
is how we found the Ford-fearing space
between smol ellipses crying wraith.
You know, that day-when you hurled
your use value at my death wish
and kissed the dew adieu,
sinus-ward and ambulatory.

Good morning: when I sing of equivalency,
it is between the spark and the sparkler;
the sorrow and the fast of it, but faster;
the polis and the rapid rate at which a body
can speed itself down the highway into
piss-black tar and other
Ballard-charmed glitters.

I tried to stop you in the street
to admire that fucking portrait
of your shoes that
you lug from bindle to back.

I tried to stop to admire
it, viz. them, viz. you,
in all the grandeur of their grandeur;
shit-stained Air Force Ones moneying the muddy sidewalk.

Walk with me for a little while
longer. I've got to tell you about when.
When you painted me for me,
my last two brain cells finally
danced celestial, terminally outsourcing
my skull for half the cost.

Delta Echo Alpha Tango Hotel;
we are pleased to meat you.

I can't the one I want have
I one the want I have can't...?
Hold on to your friends.
The thoughts are piling up—
I am only suicidal when I am
conscious of being conscious.

I wish Morrissey was more conscientious.
I wish Morrissey was dead in the flesh
all of the time so I could b'smith myself once again
and really celebrate the end of my
family hotline:
a double bed and a
fascist fucker for sure;
that's just the wretched of my poor.

There are no scalpels,
nothing cuts anymore;
nothing cuts like the way your
reams do, in essential emblems
whose episteme endeavours away the seconds
until they grow like husks in the dimmer with
each flattened LED glowing from the
midnight juices of a damp-clamped
hotdog stand—coffee, cigarettes, prismatic crises
driven by fentanyl that's surely happened somewhere
in this hospital—where I was born a double (yikes).

I want to drink you,
but I can't cum for a whole swole week.
Nothing rhymes with genitals quite like the
inedible decimals usurping incredible chemicals
in the plentiful pedestals of an ever-sicker heart;
all of your ways in the trunk of my
hunk are infected with—no future, no tutors, no booters
no no no no no no no no no no no no no no no no NO

The exactitude of this claim bobs your feet into
seas of woulda, coulda, shoulda, while exacto knives
heave their histories into the angelic splice
of United 93, unlike the way I unpack my life
over and over and—Jesus fucking Christ—over
again. While you squelch to posit songs on fife
I dismember my postal code,
again.

The real secret of this pome is that the occasion
of writing this pome is that I am sleeping off
the dregs of possible parenthoods,
sweating through a pillow and pissing my pants
through the shit of it all—goopy and
understated, I've never not recovered recoveries,
so, what has or will and will not change?

Tell me: will I be able to swallow the completeness
of my kneed-out travels if this free VPN
can take me every which where?
Am I my own daughter?

What she said: an early theft,
if that's where the trolls tractor my trailer
then what the fuck do I get?
If I only live in the past
can I squelch
            a hell yeah?

I am praying that I will be able to tell you
(in the craters of my splays)
that I am posing in my sleep again,
a squelchdaddy,
femme-ing.

No, New York (Squelching for the Red of a Hook)

New York City, huge-ass ditty—
dishing out the egomaniac's kiss,
an empirical sate of mind whose old colossus
treasures in the ancient synecdoche
of an all-pert carpet sidelining Beard Street,
where meatballs spryly fall from
the wry train of infinite resignation,
as though the city had never happened before,
its mild-wild eyes reprimanding reprimands
in the name of a monogamous nation-state,
shopping for a sectional on a date with IKEA
because it can't stand itself.

We and Me wobble to the pizza box clocktower,
devour it devoutly in low-power mode, and coax out a
synthesis of hands, kisses, and other disses with which to
heave and flip their faces toward the jade-vexed sky
and really just swish it out in the name of compacted tourism
and other formalities preceding a prolapsed protest.

It's here-where simplified filaments glissade around in
decked-out schillings to end their nine-to-fives:
grounded, sad, and tersed of squelch in overcharged
batteries, tunnels, and parks—real estate that
charges your rent rent, only to squelch into a perfectly
squared union of foolery where the grass leaves can't
predicate themselves no more.

We and Me glower to the knowledge
that all class traitors are blue without blues:
paid-out parabolas pissing out the parlance
of a skid-marked tongue, re-colonizing the land
where the pig meets the mud and the sun
meets the bun of a bodega-chopped long pome
that zounds a nation two-hundred years on.

In their bedroom before the war, it's We and Me who piss
up the city's supply of serotonin and refuse
the romantic antics of Bryant Park's Whitmanian snuff club.
If Whitman were alive today, he'd misgender them loudly

in a back booth at Stonewall and eye them like twinks
in the twinkle of his constellated horny—
fuck yeah, they'd do it, if only to remember that
queerness can't end imperialism on its own, that
this cock is a colonizer whose tip is too
speared to spare us the caprices of capital.

Any which way the eyes are in day—
it's stark as mourning when stadium lights
mutate the boulevard into biopowered
landscapes of insomniac girders,
gridding families into economies of
solar-floundered sleeplessness, mobilizing
babies into the screeching cop killers they
have only ever reamed of—
in the pang of an open, red eye,
reduction begets induction and
crime begins to rhyme with some kind of
restfulness that flexes on the margins
of third-wave coffee, laughing
at the townhomes of a next-core
gentri-fucked borough, while dedicated ouroboros
crane their thick necks to sieve out a guttural
"fuck!" at the market's arthritic paw—
it's Toronto, uncleaned; it's fascist *and* mean.

We and Me hobble into and out of the
morning of their slumber, while the city burns rubber,
ideates itself back into the closet, and
screams red alerts onto filmset squabbles. Miles away,
the downtown buildings unfetter suspired suspicions into
countersigned collected sighs, only to realize that the
post-9/11 man has always knocked twice.

They finally admit it: they can't land themselves—OW!
They offer this saxophonic truth to honour the
fractals of bridges, of buses,
and the fires they'll seize in the palimpsestual thick
of a secret buried borough birthed by those
consigned to the quenched-out words of Emma's

vandal—assemblages of rioters chuck petit bourgeois
meat and perhaps matzah balls at their origin
until the shitfuck rozzers ain't nothing but satchels
of regret, pecked to death by egrets and more
sensible comrades who gunningly puzzle out the
space between unions and thin-lined regimes.

Slacking in their slug-teethed gullets,
We and Me dig for memories of Zunes in
the dunes of a city-mold that quickly splinters into islands
of heart-things and recondite tantric antics,
unfounding paintings of nullified nexuses and
noodle-stuffed cups who signify snarls of
drummed electrolysis, plumping, instead,
for fricative fuck-faces,
brooming an unsmelt paralysis
to laugh up laps of paranoiac parodies of
their own damn industries.

On some velvet morning,
We leaves Me for a life of stolen lunch,
under the covers of a younger Jesus, who
espouses some no-name Kabbalah;
it's goth as fuck, really.
Me leaves We for the hot Hassidim who
wouldn't light a candle to their
nearly-goyish, queerly toyish ass.

That's the thing about the large apple,
everyone stems to the core an unceded
precedent for the coldness of warmth;
No New York beckons the eunoiac sconce of
No, New York while the young and dump-assed adobe slabs of
Times Square finally crumble like goat cheese
on the hook of some world-famous pie.

SQUELCH iii (Lyric for Lyrica)

The pome mirrors and mires *das kapital*,
makes *aliyah* with its own ass and
smooches everything it sees:
a thirst for terse—been there, done that;
a delet function for the baby that I am
and the comrade that I want; oof.
After a thousand retweets, some counter-vampire stuffs
the blood back in, like a coffee enema
out to munch on the complex rhythms
of a stardusted mound wearing your favourite strap-on.

The word is vital, the word is throb;
it's palindromic if you're
looking for company and need it to Be.
Does Pagliacci even eat ass?
I've only one request:
I've only one regret:
  No funeral—
  I feel great, I love sports.
  No funeral, no minyan.
Only Minion™—
this is the best I've ever felt:
I'm fitter:happier:moreproductive:
like a pig in a blanket,
a cop tethered to the upended sword-wise side
of a mop; please let me revolt myself,
I say to my revolting self.

No funeral—I'm well medicated and porous,
the pharmaceutical industrial complex has truly
shaved my life; give me another decade
to fish for some marks and *really* get it together.
But if you can't, I will once again settle
for the electricity of those eternal eateries and let
my shit turn to shan't and shun
the blue of my own reeded breath,
a system of synapses aeroplaning under
some dogged and milligram'd sea,
squelching
                    "*that's hot*: dee dee, dee dee."

```
///HhHhH//\\hahaha//\\\AaAaA\\//HhHhH//\\h
ahaha//\\\AaAaA\\//HhHhH//\\hahaha//\\\AaA
aA\\//HhHhH//\\hahaha//\\\AaAaA\\//HhHhH/
//\\hahaha//\\\AaAaA\\//HhHhH//\\hahaha//\\
\AaAaA\\//HhHhH//\\hahaha//\\\AaAaA\\//Hh
HhH//\\hahaha//\\\AaAaA\\//HhHhH//\\hahah
a//\\\AaAaA\\//HhHhH//\\hahaha//\\\AaAaA\\
///HhHhH//\\hahaha//\\\AaAaA\\//HhHhH//\\h
ahaha//\\\AaAaA\\//HhHhH//\\hahaha//\\\AaA
aA\\//HhHhH//\\hahaha//\\\AaAaA\\//HhHhH/
//\\hahaha//\\\AaAaA\\//HhHhH//\\hahaha//\\
\AaAaA\\//HhHhH//\\hahaha//\\\AaAaA\\//Hh
HhH//\\hahaha//\\\AaAaA\\//HhHhH//\\hahah
a//\\\AaAaA\\//HhHhH//\\hahaha//\\\AaAaA\\
///HhHhH//\\hahaha//\\\AaAaA\\//HhHhH//\\h
ahaha//\\\AaAaA\\//HhHhH//\\hahaha//\\\AaA
aA\\//HhHhH//\\hahaha//\\\AaAaA\\//HhHhH/
//\\hahaha//\\\AaAaA\\//HhHhH//\\hahaha//\\
\AaAaA\\//HhHhH//\\hahaha//\\\AaAaA\\//Hh
HhH//\\hahaha//\\\AaAaA\\//HhHhH//\\hahah
a//\\\AaAaA\\//HhHhH//\\hahaha//\\\AaAaA\\
///HhHhH//\\hahaha//\\\AaAaA\\//HhHhH//\\h
ahaha//\\\AaAaA\\//HhHhH//\\hahaha//\\\AaA
aA\\//HhHhH//\\hahaha//\\\AaAaA\\//HhHhH/
//\\hahaha//\\\AaAaA\\//HhHhH//\\hahaha//\\
\AaAaA\\//HhHhH//\\hahaha//\\\AaAaA\\//Hh
HhH//\\hahaha//\\\AaAaA\\//HhHhH//\\hahah
a//\\\AaAaA\\//HhHhH//\\hahaha//\\\AaAaA\\
///HhHhH//\\hahaha//\\\AaAaA\\//HhHhH//\\h
ahaha//\\\AaAaA\\//HhHhH//\\hahaha//\\\AaA
aA\\//HhHhH//\\hahaha//\\\AaAaA\\//HhHhH/
//\\hahaha//\\\AaAaA\\//HhHhH//\\hahaha//\\
\AaAaA\\//HhHhH//\\hahaha//\\\AaAaA\\//Hh
HhH//\\hahaha//\\\AaAaA\\//HhHhH//\\hahah
a//\\\AaAaA\\//HhHhH//\\hahaha//\\\AaAaA\\
```

[Sharp Squelching Sound; Jokerfication Intensifies]

When the smell is alright
and the sound pierces the sun
and all them Capricorns are caught
copper-guarding their stink with the
whitened molasses of a rubber down clink,
my whatchamacallit turns on the bright lights
in five digits or less, clenching and fisting
to face myself facing my face,
a facial façade, coming
up against its untethered smother
f.k.a. affirmations in the language of a
nauseated Levinas screaming *SMILE 4 ME.*

To smooch and to smother—
I've learned the difference in the
arrowed keys of so much
gob juice and quelled qwerty, squelching.
Having knowingly typed these lines out
a million times prior to this and prior to that,
I can shrink my teeth into the lagoon of
my seder and clap back at an eight track
playing our sound in vain—
fly me to the moon and all that.

Listen, I haven't cried in a literal decade
and it's aboutdamntime I makedamnsure
I can lock up the crocket and set myself
on fire in the spire-rhymed turnip
of cold hero soup; alphabetically,
I'm always two references away from
a wept-up storm from which
there's no going back.

I am one Mitski song away from myself,
I am an allegation against the deadest of gods (yawn),
a Tesla in the night of all probable causes,
looking some fake-ass creator in the eye and saying—
you ever try DMT, bro?
Before I trap myself in a twenty-bedroom mansion
with intent to mill.

All sadness is silly and all pomes are pissy;
I am one Waxahatchee song away from
the last words of a sharp, grass-stained hangover:
I can't escape the defensive mechanics
of loving an unlove from the furthest
breaches of a never-owned gaggle,
of a honking reticence you hear from the
window of that classroom whose song
is ten years ago: thanks, teach!

When the smell is alright,
and the dry nostrils flare,
I leave my room sighing
and crash your bicycle
into the last ravine
we ever did saw together.

I listen to myself listening to myself,
swearing allegiances to all my bodied bodies while
promising to never catfish myself again,
to never sharpen the over-hung feeling of
the all-passing morning sky. To never again
say never again, to never again gag at getting.
I look my promise in the eye and fiddle out my flawed claws:
red beams refract scratches on its singed corneas as
we absolve ourselves of silence and
slit our cakeholes some state-of-the-art smiles.
Our tattle-tapping steps uniformly shimmy us, finally,
into self-love, society, and other spit-shined
spectacles of wet hot taxidermy.

Ash-Mouth and Other Squelches

"H" – pronounced "ash" *en francais.*
"H" dawdles,
while my ass waddles
over to me on Clifton Avenue.

It's all quite
triggering.
Okay, Cixous—slow up.
Okay, Google—speed down.

The letter "H" is just boneless connectivity,
an awkward Bluetooth connection between two "I"s;
the discourse discloses itself as, no doubt,
doubtlessly, helplessly bourgeois—whatever.

Alexa, hold my beer and
sop up this tear,
I'm too weak to bake it down the stares.
Let foot fumble and flop in the name of the name
and seethe at the site of its deed—the loss of
conscience—and nest, as the flock flounders
and flubbers over the frolic.

Let me get ahold of all these
hankerings for plant rot.
It's a plight of thin-skin and tin-bone
when you Christianize me in your
edge-wedge atomicism,
re-caking my fore-signed brine into little,
red-branded eagles, American—spread
thru hoodie and thru thimble,
wrecking cons and muddying
my pissy water
asking for my son, the manager:
      it is an enlivening experience... Call It Off
      what a thrill!
Okay, Google, nudge me a little bit of your C-PTSD
and hug me with your epigenetics
so we can finally realign
my chakras.

Guided by [Squelch]es

If I waited for squelch to signify the moves that I should
make I'd go back to the lake and find another lad to eat
my matter—but who has time for that, really? On this
untapped wane of infinite solicitation, we comrades find
solace in the prehistory of sunlight, whose yum-ugly
oil slicks and vrooms us to the so-many doored stores
of Dayton in mourning, where the Second Amendment
hurricaned one too many roofs off the wings of all patrons,
pornogrinding the One-Millionth Spotlight International
into a high-up "On" position, piercing the bales of so many
lives, with peepholes aimed like aardvarks, world-sick
lasers leaping corneal into leer-teary Face-Hole, Ohio. And
yet it seems the law of love ensures everyone's insured
for a trillion living tenders, squeaking and squawking in
their dress-shooed booties, making a boogie out of every
dang thing: who would've thunk it, let alone dunked it?

I pin my nape to my fleck and buckle right up to march
our way through the high-kick flying field, where the
men are a-huffing and the prairies are a-bluffing, as
the class clown spots our UFO. Waiting for Old Uncle to
show us how it's done here, I prop myself up against the
shellacked cave whence a three-armed, space-gunned
snake comes to greet me: *I'm going to regret this, with
small courage*, slithers Pagliacci to my unimpressed face.
I scream the word out from the bird of my big boring
wedding-without-organs: Yes. The word flicks the
science right outta the pale-faced, green-mossed moon he
calls cranium. *I'm a glad girl*, I spray to the acephalous
clownsnake, I wanna get you high, make you baddest
guy on circus sign. Pagliacci replies: *Well, if that's what
you think you heard, then that's what you heard. And if
that's what you want to feel, then that's what I will sell
you.* I pick his head up off the soaring room floor, and
bunt it half-past noon, through the stratosphere.

Next on our coffee-stained plane of imminent immanence
is the doleful predilection that couples our tumblers with
a gleeful and supple howdy-do. Slaying goodbye to my
anal-retentive astrological sign, I flail colon-first into the

enchantment of some cologne found under the bushes, under the [squelch]. The radio thrums *The Days of Our Lives* for the jest of Jill Hives, milling about in a corny-cute cut-out cone of yum-slimed, slim-fasted chicken chunks in the back of a Dodge Grand Caravan I've named after the untranslatability of my thousandfold genders—so yes... thank you, next! How do you spell [squelch]? Good morrow, Old Uncle: we're off to get our wings and sing for you your droves of growers rolling by, in the trees and way below—a jar of cardinals for you to yeet and break again, then sow.

Squelch 2 Buzz (Blatting for Sweet Finity)
for J.R., into spirit

                    I imagine Emily Dickinson
imagining Joe Rosenblatt
imagining Emily Dickinson
                    imagining Joe Rosenblatt
and it's a whole lot of hmmmmmmmmmmmmmm,
when these children illegitimately endow themselves
       once-over,
umbilical c(h)ords tickling a pinch of honey-slipped
retroactivities and archival proclivities,
a bio-lack strapped to the lick of their grinch,
buzzing bites through socialist space-time:
ketchup, mustard, relish, drones, prayer—
oh, Emily! Oh, Joe! The condiments are yours.
Take heed—they are but mommapapas de-conforming,
hmmmmmmmmmmmmmming with heaves of
fricked frictionals—otherwise hyperstitional
in the deep-spaced reel of yearly et ceteras,
engendering multitudes of em-dashed weaponry
and page-plucked, glottal sorcery.
Whose loon ticks more in the night
of a muse-born square-dance with wings a-bumbling?
Who dares pray with unanswered believers? O! it's just
       J & Em,
jambing for honey.
Solar-hued insects nourish the blues,
hijacking a hijacker in lo-fi velocities,
busily occupied, clustering, reeking of havoc and
other love poems. Joe leagues for the jeers
against some Miltonic diatribe—it's all strategy,
it's all buzziness, and Canada blesses
his Talmudic shoulders with some honey, and a few apples,
but it's never enough or enough—of never.

Our bubbies do fuzz a tussock of cause,
nuzzling off the snazzers with rozzers
in the razzers of a post-hazard cookout, the remnants of
a Face screeching for a neo-Seder within and without that
"Hamburger Helper called Post-Modernism."
What's dogmatic secularity if not a mystical could-be?

78

A basic and beefy worker bee hardening its union knees
in the upper of an intellection telethon funding another
     Cuban
Revolution, unloading boxcars with sustained levity,
a milkshake shaking with the thought of
Marx buzzing Lenin buzzing Trotsky—thanks again, see
     ya!
The *torat hayim* is a summer in Allan, gardening
so much fun from an SPF 50-covered stun
while six and a million folks beat those fuckos to
a pulp, glossing community. Oh, so the bees are circumcised,
     Al?
Manic shoppers, burglars of the soul are
cross-pollinating and topping elephant fetishists—
so many shrivelled sweet peas, a Judaic
undertow that you can't knock over
with a pail of holy water. An Acorn acronym splays
to the earth, like mommapapa at the MOMA
on a bleached-out Sunday at Qualicum:
a day's worth of a day's worth is seeking the comradery
of shells and smells and other buccal buccaneers to offer
     Kaddish—
well, here goes a gnostic Gnothing.

Our lives are Swiss and all bees are gymnasts
rising out to roar out a root when Emily
sashays for Joe and Joe-dashes-for-Em,
blipping that proteins are best absorbed
when our rives are rotisserie'd by tender fingers
buttoning erasers to the slickness of an apiary.
The parabellum coagulates at the bottom of your barrel,
     loaded.
Like a nun, hymning and hmmmmmmmmmmmmmming
through the tempest of a green and
weathered shul. The hives bleat out the League of Canadian
     Poets
and throws it into the sucrose sweat
of Georgia's Strait: no no   I've almost forgotten
the BOSS QUEEN and the way an apiary

79

can be so 🐝 slick and real 🐝 🐝 🐝 🐝 🐝
the way a bee can grace us with a sting
and lay 🐝 🐝 waste to the distance it permeates.
Oh, Joe, it's off to the to-fro, where, from Emily and 🐝 🐝 🐝 🐝
suchlike company, you continue to buzz in the syrup 🐝 🐝 🐝 🐝 🐝
of a socialist glow 🐝 🐝 🐝 🐝 🐝 🐝, foaming out the dew of a duly-
    dialed due:
🐝 i miss you [BOSS QUEEN]; i love you 🐝 [BOSS QUEEN],
                adieu, [BOSS QUEEN], adieu, adieu
🐝 — 🐝

Holding Space for Me, My[Squelch], & I

i love you [space bar]
love you [space bar]
ove you [space bar]
ve you [space bar]
e you [space bar]
you [space bar]
ou [space bar]
u [space bar]
[space bar]
space bar]
pace bar]
ace bar]
ce bar]
e bar]
bar]
ar]
r]
]

i
i l
i lo
i lov
i love
i love y
i love yo
i love you
i love you [
i love you [s
i love you [sp
i love you [spa
i love you [spac
i love you [space
i love you [space b
i love you [space ba
i love you [space bar
i love you [space bar]

Predicative Predictions (Siri Squelch)

I'm sorry to say I am sorry for your long text sorry to say that you were going well but also I am sorry to miss y'all but I'm gonna was a great time for ya and you were going well so sorry to say I love y'all

I'm so sorry to say that this I'm so glad y'all got the time I'm sorry I didn't wanna talk about I'm so glad y'all got the I'm so sorry to say I am I'm so sorry I forgot I'm so glad I wanna I'm so sorry I wanna is I'm sorry to say I'm so glad I wanna

Dear I am not going on the way that you were gonna last year we had some fun and we were just trying not gonna it is so fun omg is that the one I love that I wanna is a great time for ya and you for ya know what you mean gotta is was that meme way day was so great is the a I was the I didn't know get back in to you I only wanted got to go the night today

So, Thus a Lilith Squelch (For Skin & Eschaton)

The mutter muttered them from community. (So, thus), a bat, a hearse, and no manner. No matter. Napped, no kidding, by the knave. Overwrought, frightened-in-a-word. Cut them from their cutting. More cutting, more and more cutting until the sore rung bore, while lifes did sing. Endless, but the button did shine. The button upon blazer, old friends of the feed, stones who tear up alongside the weepy wimp, hand-in-tongue and sober still, not snide. Cranks by the button-head, the gnarl near to suffocate. In their haste, nearly unnoticed. The toddler toddling without sod, weeply nibbling at the bodice. They, screech owl. Arms outstretched to carry fast with rank strength the blooméd wings in morning.[PISS]

Stepped into the car—driving off any which way, somehow, sighless (so, thus), into sun, which stoned its shine. As did eyes in feigned vista; a van in miniature, without sunroof nor sod nor tray in which to ash or fasten. Bland-gray upholstered gummings upon which asses keep kempt of bondage in time and certitude, firmly. Alack, for a dearth of belts and seats to go with aged edge and moisture wreathing bedside stench, fleas to snore, between the toddles of carseat lock and lore. A night-hoot, without rapport.[MISS]

What remains of the fore, this Rembrandt, [is] torn into small, very regular squares and rammed down Elijah's chair: ass to nuzzle fair in lair, yes, the heart unsized, divined into two, yes, the kissing and/or hissing in their winking twinkdom, yes. What's twenty years if not the mend, sealing, unsealing, circumscribing locks of hair-moss posing 'round the rim and/or rosary, onward leading the wander, by and by, a mezuzah-flocked snare. Crouched there, lapping up the lap, face first into speaking, their hymn and its imminence, in their it, conjuring abruption. The bespattered mess of ten thousand fools abroad. The runes of a Saturday

---

PISS I Will Always Miss You
MISS I Will Always Miss

made nigh as night dawns its starry imprint, veiling a face, or Talmud.^{KISS}

    For a Jew (so, thus) is one inwardly & not by the letter.^{HISS}

---

^{KISS}   I Will Always

^{HISS}   "Then when she breathed her last, the boy Adeodatus cried out in sorrow and was pressed by all of us to be silent. In this way too something of the child in me, which had slipped towards weeping, was checked and silenced by the youthful voice.

Digression III: Discourse on the Other Side of Scream-Heart

Hi, mommy. Open your mouth. Say awwww.
Did you know that

The messiah will come only when [They]
is no longer necessary;
[They] will come only on the day
after [Their] arrival;
[They] will come
not on the last day,
but on the very last.
?
You can tell me,
it's okay, haha.
But right now, us girls
just wanna have fun.

Why don't you mound up the number you most proffer and
set your watch to decimate; get yourself to sleep for once,
lest you get too dizzy with dementia!
I don't want another all-nighter—
G-d forbid, we're not first in line for
the Ghoster Coaster, swiftly cancelled
for our boasting.

While blossoms supplant your burnt-out arnicas,
take another toke and eradicate me, why dontcha?
I know our house stands wooden on its coccyx, its forbidden
      pleas,
under rouses of sleep hygiene which reluctantly enable me
to see the way I say my own name in the mirror—
booping and bopping, all shivery-nimble, flacked into
closed-mouth rivers, molting scarves in their wetness
right outta my shoulders, miming miniatures as particulate as
the particles whose nebulae make my maker meet my mead:
apples and honey, honey.

But please, just let us go.
I need to hear the angels n the debbils sing:
Welcome to Wonderland,
there is no exit.

I kiss my inner child on his four-headed forehead and
launch his ancestors decades worth of future, blank into
    the mud,
slugging mommy through the telephone with a sing-song
by Barry Manilow we knew once nary well.
Don't worry, *I'll look after him,* I tell her
but she smells the lie and sicks me with it later.

I rush and I hush to clean up the mush;
I hang up, nervous and crushed.
I call us a taxi but wish for a bus.
Our cinder goes asunder and before you sow it,
we're all lawned out, whooping our coughs
all over the ass of Behemoth's green mantle.

On the other side of the mauve-clapped grass,
mommy insurrects my ideologies while I suck a
flash of Flintstone'd wonder; the mommy still
running her Mcluhan-esque mouth, leaking
screams no heart could contain,
spreading that mommy love—
spectacular, mawkish, covering
lineup after lineup with lime-flavoured dread,
the embarrassment of well-intentioned credit cards
maxing their lax on the bellows of hacks—
generational, wistful, dramatic traumatics,
laying pipes of overkill beneath the piped-down
animatronics who stare at
me and mine, pointing and laughing.

I let my inner child wound himself with all the chili a
dog could muster on a hot summer's day; he sprays off the
vomit in the mist of Mountain Dew's very own
autonomous zone, and then:
boom, some other Anthropocene Brexits
through the gift shop, evacuates its bowels face-first
as a reminder to all us simps that we must
keep warm and stay safe,
fawn flames, and hope that our gingko trees may
sweat these forevers into the fresh of a flesh-meshed never.

We'll know it by the heart, grabbing us through the throat—
a scream by any other name wouldn't, couldn't, shouldn't
smell as sweet as our sleeping giant, snoring economy,
watching children march deathward into re-educated
    dreams,
drumming on about no turning at any point,
no back to fall back on, snoring louder,
a gingko, blooming in reverse,
snoring language like chili dogs
dripping in the heat of
an open mouth, closing.

Puckering Sambation and Pissing the Jeans (Squelching at Mount Royal)
before A.M. Klein

Poetry incests us emotionally;
it foresees and climbs deeply
a tree, where finally we
brush-to-tarry and bury the
cortisonal cup of curbed-up
Xanax, fop, and, so it is written,
brie.

A warble we left
tipped at the fresh of the crave is still
percolating old tongues from
the Chemex and the coal
we heaved off a branch,
who sank our messiah
into the heat
six blocks ago:
baby lawns and Babylons—
henlo Leonard, a-dieu Kohen
we hope you enjoy our
fidget spinner's Kaddish
for now it is time
to share us a hiss,
at the base of this mountain
we nag and submiss.

Est-ce que je peux aller aux toilettes
is a grade school monolingualism
sacking around the metro until the tills
cramp forward for a wish from the
fair inspector's entire family,
who are convinced,
no, really, he's a good guy, a
slack soldier dreaming
conniption to hog
us all to bells.

As per usual, don't @ me.
As per my email, don't @ me.
I just need you to
spell it for me: YHWH,
that earnest ear of corn
refrigerating a whole host of
air and BnBs
on the very last syllabus of all
drubbed beginnings,
dotting too many anglo asses with
excessive doubleyous who rummage
the grain elevator for sustainability and
political meetings after silent discos
in your dumped-about yard-back;
but not tonight, instead, we've a yet-again'd
question of time dressed in et ceteras
bumping mouth-tight umbrellas
in a day sly as desert:
a clapped shot of landscape as poet,
        squelching in squalled haptics
        for a foraged mode of portrait, asking—
                "wouldn't you like to know it?"

SQUELCH iv (Back Up the Ashes on a Flash Drive)

Ada Lovelace sitting in a tree,
techne, zero, one and me.
They're all my friends, and me.
It's playtime on G-d's clean floor, where
nearby rivers squelch collectively—
all-knowing punks,
coursing through courses,
posting bills for
those who remain.
This breath of water is
antiboomer aktion,
the kind of cake you don't serve your mother.
You don't serve her anything,
really. You pull back the poster,
whistling for a razorblade.
It's a brevity in levity,
an indirection chalking perfection up to itself.
A satanic hologram touring
widespread theses,
swirling the optics of a beach-blonde soup,
while I callous the heroes from my feet
off the shore of this campus.
On the board
you find a safe self,
whose wounds favoured quiescence
and sealed themselves shut.
Home is in Sadie's puck-welping face
buried in the pillow,
not looking at me,
stripping your nakedness of itself,
as though there were
ninety-five of her, all
panting and purring,
thetic and pawing the door
with an animal's smile—truly
the truth of truth, a
snug-slugged fido
for philosophy.
To her, you're a thing amongst others,
thinging along on G-d's clean floor,
like a coffee cup, barking up the heat.

Quiet Roads Fulla Sicko Odes
(Squelched Confessional)

There was a time
when meadow,
grove, and stream,
the earth, and every common sight, to me did seem
apparelled in celestial plight, flowing into
sicko mode, with a dousing or two of an
old Lysolian brew and a few thousand bucks for
some hot minutes of low-flying complacency,
maiming the way to encircle
face (yours) in hands (mine),
from distances both social and gleaming
with words of sassed and sacred molasses,
charming out freedom from chasms, and screaming:
time is a flat circle identical to a snake
eating its own ass, a lovence made rye
and brain-fried with a side of
"oh, hi," says a kleptomaniac out for a walk on the
    morning of some
super Tuesday yet-to-come—a justified and true
Tree of Knowledge, whose throne whelps both
coccyx and phalanx, pissing askance at itself
from Augusta to Dufferin, practicing the words and the
    script
that could make a golem outta one-billion discarded
    masks and
and a lipstick-red smiley face.

What can we make of a time whose tell
ticks to the teat of so many death knells?
Are we merely pog-pilled Jokers, lost
like jeers in rain, unfit for singularity in "we"?
Indooby-doobitubly.

A virus is a language outing the space of its pace,
squelching in the flare-up of solar anuses, rapidly
aging the gobsmacked looks off our
G-d-sacked faces, lamenting lamentations:
send Tweet and psalm another gob,
find a one-bathroom loft of your own,
write the same story a thousand times over,
hack into the nodal network of all possible affects

formerly known as Studio Ghibli,
listen to Animal Collective—oh, to Be again!

But now it is time to stink off the
obliviousness of obvious oblivions and
niff ourselves of petulance, depression, anxiety,
derealities, quaffed normalities, traumatic complexities—
whatever it takes to eclipse the apex of this fold,
be it the wreckage of my sweat-dressed Lexapro,
or all those quips (protective and personal)
it takes to block out some avatar, nude and
in the making, whose tongue runs rungs
twenty miles away at two-thousand miles an hour.

Now, every time I sneeze,
I'm a monster by mistake,
frantically Googling parental obits,
asking Siri to dream
of those good old days when words meant their worth
and the noontime moon struck twice to wind taut and
to tote its own watch:
first as raggedy, then as a lark,
cracking the skull of
an aporetic soup can.

Notwithstanding, all the youngsters dug heel to hope
in the hype of it all, forgetting the
malarkey of every past, present, and realtor'd future,
those ancestral whatchamacallits—
you know the thing you thought would
make all the Joes of the world finally disappear—
too bad! It's much more unforgivable
than that.

A gathering of more than two but no less
than ten may wreck the barrel of this border,
its gauze encasements, and forevermore
knot it with the throat-back of a
well-hung lung amongst a flush of clots.

In feverous dreams, sifting through my archive,
ma-ma-ma my mommy tells me she ain't

gonna make it, tells me her last words ought to be:
a virus is a language from outer space,
tattooed on the wrist of a wrangly Warren staffer,
touching faces and spitting in the mouths of wide-open
        rabbis,
asking for the manager, complaining about all these
bad vibes, pondering which brand of eugenics
could realign the chakras of an ideology "without history"—
but maybe I should just ask my accountant.
Now listen here, Jack:
        To me the meanest flower that blows can give
        Thoughts that do often lie too deep for tears:

iTsOkAyToNoTbEoKaY
iTsOkAyToNoTbEoKaY
iTsOkAyToNoTbEoKaY
iTsOkAyToNoTbEoKaY
iTsOkAyToNoTbEoKaY
iTsOkAyToNoTbEoKaY
iTsOkAyToNoTbEoKaY
iTsOkAyToNoTbEoKaY
iTsOkAyToNoTbEoKaY
iTsOkAyToNoTbEoKaY
iTsOkAyToNoTbEoKaY

So, let's respire cronyisms
until we're heavy as a well,
clasping simpers to the silence
of our big mushy hotheads,
while our lungs lick light,
pulsating to the knowledge that
beyond Sambation, a speedway is
sulking in its quietude,
wearing thin in the thick
of an ode it squelches to the sick,
in absentia, off,

                and ticked.

Every Little Kiss is Pleading for Kaddish
after Leonard Cohen

You do not do, you do not do anymore, blue Jews—for whom
I have lived like soot in a tarried foot's worth of burnt
offerings.
With and without you, I'm going AWOL, kaputting old
selves
betwixt the muscle and the coffee, where I gleam of you,
dead daddies—
of your grease and tomfoolery, your citations and jewelry—
dead daddies, no no no, I really did not not not want you to
go! But you
squelched before I had time to hiss out a kiss—in tongue
and in tonsil and in piss—
for those fistfuls of dialectics you'd so sneezily zap into a
zayde's worth
of bearded dianetics, through the brooding cult of bedrooms,
billing and cooing,
haunting the sap between each step toward an ancient
clear. In the pace of my gait,
made randy by the frankness of psalms, I am gobbing and
grinding you into my phone
until my toe pricks the shoe right through its foggéd bough
and
we all fall blat into empty metro; petals, wet, black, and
hacking at
futures you had thrice sowed, whose coughs are only ever
masques of themselves—oh.
Dead daddies, I have had to bill you for the time you stole
domming my
nervous system with pectoral runabouts, putting mouth to
grunt where
my sun oughta live to spit shine another day; enough is
enough!
We are young, hummed, and full of cumbrous
methodologies for waking up on walk-ups of multiplexed
scrolls,
sleuthing to print, hex, and gnash incestuous our gnostic
rouse.
Dead daddies, I have always been scared of you, your bold-
leaded heads

94

squelching genealogy, dumping crumb for crumb:

a vers for a vice who could never play nice.

Dead daddies, I'd love to leave my memories by the rinds of

a puddle named Sambation, at the base of Mount Royal,

where I left my fidget spinning in the dusk of your
    yesterdays, on that

tusk of a morning during which you scoffed, finally, that
    messiahs are as

gooey as marmalade—masticating noshes likes sieves in
    the night;

that diaspora belongs to no one; that we no longer long for
    belonging,

that an arm can flex in safety and caffeinate its degeneracy,

swaying to the bawdy of our knowledge without irruption.

No longer can we see the difference between a pome and a
    handshake,

but still must I pray that you, in horny matrimony, went so
    far as to peck

your way toward another, gayer Abraham—only then can
    we imagine ourselves happy.

Oh, dead daddies, you strung out my genders to dry in
    the sky and clipped yourselves so many Hitlers for a
    single flower; camping oxidation like small smiles at
    the bottom of my sea.

Oh, dead daddies—I know that I don't owe it, but I am
    dancing and stamping with you.

Dead daddies, you tightropes, I'm—Who?

THIS PAGE INTENTIONALLY LEFT [SQUELCHED]
THIS PAGE INTENTIONALLY LEFT [SQUELCHED]
THIS PAGE INTENTIONALLY LEFT [SQUELCHED]
THIS PAGE INTENTIONALLY LEFT [SQUELCHED]
THIS PAGE INTENTIONALLY LEFT [SQUELCHED]
THIS PAGE INTENTIONALLY LEFT [SQUELCHED]
THIS PAGE INTENTIONALLY LEFT [SQUELCHED]
THIS PAGE INTENTIONALLY LEFT [SQUELCHED]
THIS PAGE INTENTIONALLY LEFT [SQUELCHED]
THIS PAGE INTENTIONALLY LEFT [SQUELCHED]
THIS PAGE INTENTIONALLY LEFT [SQUELCHED]
THIS PAGE INTENTIONALLY LEFT [SQUELCHED]
THIS PAGE INTENTIONALLY LEFT [SQUELCHED]
THIS PAGE INTENTIONALLY LEFT [SQUELCHED]
THIS PAGE INTENTIONALLY LEFT [SQUELCHED]
THIS PAGE INTENTIONALLY LEFT [SQUELCHED]
THIS PAGE INTENTIONALLY LEFT [SQUELCHED]
THIS PAGE INTENTIONALLY LEFT [SQUELCHED]
THIS PAGE INTENTIONALLY LEFT [SQUELCHED]
THIS PAGE INTENTIONALLY LEFT [SQUELCHED]
THIS PAGE INTENTIONALLY LEFT [SQUELCHED]
THIS PAGE INTENTIONALLY LEFT [SQUELCHED]
THIS PAGE INTENTIONALLY LEFT [SQUELCHED]
THIS PAGE INTENTIONALLY LEFT [SQUELCHED]
THIS PAGE INTENTIONALLY LEFT [SQUELCHED]
THIS PAGE INTENTIONALLY LEFT [SQUELCHED]
THIS PAGE INTENTIONALLY LEFT [SQUELCHED]
THIS PAGE INTENTIONALLY LEFT [SQUELCHED]
THIS PAGE INTENTIONALLY LEFT [SQUELCHED]
THIS PAGE INTENTIONALLY LEFT [SQUELCHED]
THIS PAGE INTENTIONALLY LEFT [SQUELCHED]
THIS PAGE INTENTIONALLY LEFT [SQUELCHED]
THIS PAGE INTENTIONALLY LEFT [SQUELCHED]
THIS PAGE INTENTIONALLY LEFT [SQUELCHED]
THIS PAGE INTENTIONALLY LEFT [SQUELCHED]
THIS PAGE INTENTIONALLY LEFT [SQUELCHED]

```
///HhHhH///boo\\\hahaha///who\\\\AaAaA\\\//////H
hHhH///boo\\\hahaha///who\\\\AaAaA\\\//////HhH
hH///boo\\\hahaha///who\\\\AaAaA\\\//////HhHhH/
//boo\\\hahaha///who\\\\AaAaA\\\//////HhHhH//bo
o\\\hahaha///who\\\\AaAaA\\\//////HhHhH//boo\\\
hahaha///who\\\\AaAaA\\\//////HhHhH//boo\\\ha
haha///who\\\\AaAaA\\\//////HhHhH//boo\\\haha
ha///who\\\\AaAaA\\\//////HhHhH//boo\\\hahaha/
//who\\\\AaAaA\\\//////HhHhH//boo\\\hahaha///w
ho\\\\AaAaA\\\//////HhHhH//boo\\\hahaha///who\
\\\\AaAaA\\\//////HhHhH//boo\\\hahaha///who\\\\A
aAaA\\\//////HhHhH//boo\\\hahaha///who\\\\AaAa
A\\\//////HhHhH//boo\\\hahaha///who\\\\AaAaA\\\
//////HhHhH//boo\\\hahaha///who\\\\AaAaA\\\/////
/HhHhH//boo\\\hahaha///who\\\\AaAaA\\\//////Hh
HhH//boo\\\hahaha///who\\\\AaAaA\\\//////HhHh
H//boo\\\hahaha///who\\\\AaAaA\\\//////HhHhH//
boo\\\hahaha///who\\\\AaAaA\\\//////HhHhH//boo
\\\hahaha///who\\\\AaAaA\\\//////HhHhH//boo\\\h
ahaha///who\\\\AaAaA\\\//////HhHhH//boo\\\haha
ha///who\\\\AaAaA\\\//////HhHhH//boo\\\hahaha/
//who\\\\AaAaA\\\//////HhHhH//boo\\\hahaha///w
ho\\\\AaAaA\\\//////HhHhH//boo\\\hahaha///who\
\\\\AaAaA\\\//////HhHhH//boo\\\hahaha///who\\\\A
aAaA\\\//////HhHhH//boo\\\hahaha///who\\\\AaAa
A\\\//////HhHhH//boo\\\hahaha///who\\\\AaAaA\\\
//////HhHhH//boo\\\hahaha///who\\\\AaAaA\\\/////
/HhHhH//boo\\\hahaha///who\\\\AaAaA\\\//////Hh
HhH//boo\\\hahaha///who\\\\AaAaA\\\//////HhHh
H//boo\\\hahaha///who\\\\AaAaA\\\//////HhHhH//
boo\\\hahaha///who\\\\AaAaA\\\//////HhHhH//boo
\\\hahaha///who\\\\AaAaA\\\//////HhHhH//boo\\\h
ahaha///who\\\\AaAaA\\\//////HhHhH//boo\\\haha
ha///who\\\\AaAaA\\\//////HhHhH//boo\\\hahaha/
//who\\\\AaAaA\\\//////HhHhH//boo\\\hahaha///w
ho\\\\AaAaA\\\//////HhHhH//boo\\\hahaha///who\
\\\\AaAaA\\\//////HhHhH//boo\\\hahaha///who\\\\A
aAaA\\\//////HhHhH//boo\\\hahaha///who\\\\AaAa
A\\\//////HhHhH//boo\\\hahaha///who\\\\AaAaA\\\
//////HhHhH//boo\\\hahaha///who\\\\AaAaA\\\/////
/HhHhH//boo\\\hahaha///who\\\\AaAaA\\\//////Hh
HhH//boo\\\hahaha///who\\\\AaAaA\\\//////HhHh
```

ACKNOWLEDGE[SQUELCH]

Henlo and welcome to the end of [SQUELCH PROCEDURES] by MLA Chernoff. Thank you for reading [SQUELCH PROCEDURES] by MLA Chernoff—that's real noice of you, wowee UwU o.O

This book was a laborious labour of loving love for the love of love. I would like to thank the following friendos for their support over the years, either before, during, or after the composition of this book—y'all are wonderful and inspiring in your own magical ways. I honour you and I honour the squelch called "friendship" that, together, we have cultivated: Vannessa Barnier, Gary Barwin, bill bissett, Lauren Fournier, Emil Hastymart, Adam Kamin, Zak Jones, Adeena Karasick, Sophie McCreesh, Fawn Parker, Eric Schmaltz, Kate Siklosi, Dani Spinosa, Katherine Walker-Jones, and Peach Travis Waluigi.

I am also grateful for the kindness, generosity, and fruitful insight of the team at Gordon Hill Press: Shane Neilson and Jeremy Luke Hill. Thank you for giving this book a chance to live, laugh, and love.

Earlier versions of various squelches have had the privilege of appearing in *Bad Dog Review, Bad Nudes, Half a Grapefruit, Peach Mag,* rob mclennan's *Spotlight and Tuesday Dusie, Train: A Poetry Journal,* and *Trash Magazine.* Truly the validation I needed to keep writing and existing—big thanks!

Best wishes & cheers & love to you all in bittersweet sol,

MLA Chernoff
01/05/2021
xo xo
bottom text

About MLA CHERNOFF

MLA Chernoff (they/them/@squelch_bb) was born at Women's College Hospital in December of 1991—oops. They are a six-hundred-year-old Jewish, non-binary pome machine, a Postmodern Neo-Marxist, and (somehow) a PhD Candidate at the Neoliberal University of York University, where they once held a SSHRC Doctoral Fellowship— no kidding. They would like to recall a slightly edited version of their first widely published "bio," featured in *Bad Nudes*, Issue 2.1:

> MLA Chernoff hacks, lacks, and really needs you to cut them some slack(s). They are the fullness of a floor-swept boredom: dusted, through and through. Their pomes have been featured in ditch, The Hart House Review, AND Acta Victoriana, AND angelfire.com. MLA Chernoff lives in Toronto and (naïvely) believes in love and/or/as resentment. The velocity of this bio is their dissertation—a thanatropic tepidity in the key "dang."

That was quite nice; MLA thanks you for reading about one of their former selves. In any and all cases, MLA now has IBS (Irritable Bowel Syndrome), as well as a few more publications both under and over their "belt": their first chapbook, *delet this*, was released by Bad Books in 2018. Their second collection, *TERSE THIRSTY*, was released by Gap Riot Press in 2019. MLA has also been featured in *The Bad Dog Review, Peach Mag, Spam Zine, Train, Trash Magazine*, and other loveable publications. What a wild ride it's been for them! They are currently spewing out a sequel to *TERSE THIRSTY*, entitled *TONGUE HUNGRY*, but most of all, they are taking time to work on themself. MLA would like to add that they are a settler living, working, kissing, and hissing in Tkaronto, particularly in Treaty 13 territory.